Testimonials

I had an opportunity to interact with Dr Bindu Selot when I started my business venture, Eurokids Preschool. My first interaction with her was an eye opener, not only to the world of preschoolers, but also about recruitment of teachers, their orientation and professional development trainings, as well as handling of parents and children. She ignited my passion as a preschool educator and care giver.

The teachers' and parents' workshops conducted by her at my centre were a great learning experience for me. The way she sensitized me has enabled me to connect to my preschoolers, my teachers and my parents. She has been a mentor who was handholding me with so much love, care and knowledge and helped me discover my sense of purpose.

Her initiatives of reaching out to the society with her books, workshops and counselling sessions are a blessing to parents and educators.

Vinita Kala, Principal and Owner,
Eurokids, Dehradun

As a teacher, you were the first person who trusted me, who had faith in my abilities. Slowly, you brought me out of my cocoon and gave me the faith that I only had to spread my wings and the sky can be mine. You told me that I have to have faith in myself and believe in myself much before anyone else believed in me.

As a teacher, you became my role model. I always try to follow your footsteps. You have been my guiding light, my anchor—always.

Anjali Prakash, Science Teacher,
Central Academy, Lucknow

Your guru mantra for handling kids gave me the vision in my career to understand the kids better emotionally and psychologically, and in imparting education to them holistically, paving the path for more practical based learning. As a mentor, you also taught me how to handle teachers, understand them and empathize with them, to create a healthy team spirit and collaborative working.

Kaushiki Das, *Junior Headmistress,*
Delhi International School, Dwarka, New Delhi

Through your training and mentoring, I was able to mould myself as an individual with a persona to influence and serve the society. You, as my teacher, not only nurtured my skills but also helped me discover my hidden abilities, which I am proud of. With your incredible techniques, you are one of the finest teachers I have been blessed with.

Aman Sehgal, *Consultant Physiotherapist,*
Fitness and Diet Consultant, Delhi

To me, you have been a real mentor and a great guide. You have helped me understand relationship management, developing self-confidence, understanding the powers of the universe and the law of attraction, which I am using on a daily basis. My life went through a lot of ups and downs, but with your mentoring, I was confident and emotionally stable. I could handle everything with grace. I owe my settled life and the present calmness to you because of your special words and guidance. The affirmations provided by you were of real help in gaining the positivity in my life. I owe this happiness to you. I feel blessed to have you as my best teacher and mentor. Thanks for being there Ma'am — a big gratitude.

Mandakini Chopra, *Senior Physiotherapist & Patient Care Officer,*
Portea Medical, Delhi-NCR

It has been a privilege to be your student. Not only were your classes a respite from the usual monotonous professional lectures, there was an element of realism in your sessions. You are my idol for the art and science called "teaching". You are a teacher for life. It is a matter of pride to be mentored by you. Ma'am, you are an inspiration at all times. Keep rocking!

Divya Gupta, Paediatric Physiotherapist,
New Delhi

Thank you Ma'am, for teaching me those basic essentials of life which became the core of my foundation and helped me figure out who I am, what I am capable of and how to frame the goals of my life and achieve them. I still remember your first lecture, where I got the first lesson of my life from you. From then till now, I have seen lots of ups and downs, stood up alone for the right—against all odds, faced all the obstacles with a smile, walked down rough roads, knowing that no one can change my values. You are a true teacher, who has helped me walk on the right path, taught me to walk with pride, to never be afraid of setting high goals.

Lipi Verma, Senior Physiotherapist and Clinical Quality Manager,
AKtiv Ortho, Delhi

You are an outstanding counsellor and trainer, who has empowered students and colleagues alike. I have developed a special friendship and a meaningful relationship with you, which has enriched both my personal as well as my professional life.

You are an elegant speaker and a master of unique words. Each of your sessions created feelings of strength, positivity and belief in me, which helped me to become a better teacher and a better human being. Thank you, Dr Bindu, for always being there.

Gagan Kaur Thukral,
Amiown School, Pushp Vihar, New Delhi

My life totally changed after attending your classes. The classes not only transformed me into a better teacher, but also helped in enlightening my spirits within. Now I am a successful teacher at a reputed school and, for me, each child is unique. My sincere gratitude to you, Bindu Ma'am.

Deepika Sethi, Primary Teacher,
Hillwoods Academy, Delhi

Being your student was an amazing experience. I am falling short of words to thank you and appreciate the beauty of the most influential and informative psychology classes I have ever been to. I feel this has given me enough to explore my views and has also made me a lot more interested about experimenting with new methods in teaching.

Absolutely wonderful and transformational were your classes. Not only did the experience provide me with an opportunity to add value to the lives of students, but it also provided me the opportunity to grow and learn more about myself as a person. I feel so enriched, and I am sure to enrich the school where I teach.

As your student, I felt like a sponge absorbing every bit of information I could. Everything I did was immediately applicable to my classes and my students. Thank you so much, Ma'am, for what you have taught me. I came as a trainee and walked away as an evolved educator.

Kavita Negi, PRT,
Sardar Patel Vidyalaya, New Delhi

You are a true guide, motivator and a mentor to me. You have helped me to understand my true calibre by introducing me to my real self. Thank you, Ma'am, for inculcating the value of being a democratic facilitator, rather than being a regular teacher.

Deepti Nair, Teacher,
Global Indian International School, Noida

As a Psychology Professor, you have inspired me for the energy and passion that I required to understand my students. I have read both your books, which have beautiful anecdotes which are so relevant for handling children and their behaviour. The books have been an immense referral point for me, for not only in understanding my own children, but also in understanding the children I teach. I continue to read your blogs, which are so well expressed.

Pallavi Tomar, Pre Primary Teacher,
Amity International School, Noida

You are not just a good teacher, you are one of the kind every student might have only aspired to have. You are a friend, philosopher and guide. You changed my perspective of parenting and teaching. From being the tiger mum, I became a participative parent and a non-judgemental teacher. Your sessions were most engaging and we always asked for more.

Lavanya, On-site Coordinator,
Melbourne, Australia

You put your heart, mind and soul in teaching your students. You are humble, passionate, skilful and teach from your personal experience. As a student, I have imbibed the right values from you that will stay with me for life. Besides being one of the finest teachers I have had, you are a friend, philosopher and guide. I am truly grateful to you.

Julie, a passionate, full-time Mom,
New Delhi

For me, you are the Sun and I am a planet revolving around you for learning, on a daily basis. The warmth, the knowledge and the teaching I received from you has enabled me to spread happy smiles on the faces of kids all around.

Suneeta Mohanty, Teacher,
Takshila School, Bhubaneswar

Let Me Make A Difference

Mom & Dad

Road map for every teacher's success

Let Me Make A Difference
Mom & Dad
Road map for every teacher's success

Dr Bindu Selot

STERLING PAPERBACKS
An imprint of
Sterling Publishers (P) Ltd.
Regd. Office: A1/256 Safdarjung Enclave,
New Delhi-110029. Cin: U22110DL1964PTC211907
Tel: 26387070, 26386209; Fax: 91-11-26383788
E-mail: mail@sterlingpublishers.com
www.sterlingpublishers.com

Let Me Make a Difference, Mom & Dad
© 2016, Dr Bindu Selot
ISBN 978 93 85913 99 0

All rights are reserved.
No part of this publication may be reproduced, stored in a retrieval system or transmitted, in any form or by any means, mechanical, photocopying, recording or otherwise, without prior written permission of the author.

Printed in India

Printed and Published by Sterling Publishers Pvt. Ltd.,
Plot No. 13, Ecotech-III, Greater Noida - 201306,
Uttar Pradesh, India

Dedication

I dedicate this book to all the teachers who I have come across during this beautiful journey of my life.

These are the teachers who have taught me, the teachers who have taught my children, the teachers who have been my colleagues, all the teachers with whom I have been interacting during my trainings and workshops, the teachers who have come to me for counselling and, above all, the trainee teachers of Amity Centre for Educational Research and Training (ACERT), who have been my very enthusiastic students and have always inspired me to write down my thoughts. Each one of you, dear teachers, has contributed in the making of this book.

Thank you, God, for enriching my life with such an eclectic mix of teachers. I feel truly blessed to be a Teacher-Trainer, a practising Parent Counsellor and an author. My passionate vision is to sensitize the teaching fraternity by sharing my learnings through this book that you are holding in your hand, because you, dear teachers, are impacting the children for life.

Acknowledgements

First of all, I would like to thank Mr S. K Ghai, Managing Director, Sterling Publishers Pvt. Ltd., for that call which he made to ask me if I would be interested in writing a book on skill development. I immediately grabbed the opportunity and said an instant "Yes" to him and also shared that I wanted to write a book for teachers.

In fact, I had already been considering an idea of writing a book for teachers for long. So there has been no looking back after that. I was already enthused about the book and Mr Ghai's enthusiasm, motivation, and belief in me made the journey of writing this book immensely meaningful. A very special thanks to all his staff members for their unconditional support in the publishing of this book.

Nothing can be complete without my special thanks to my editor, Mr Sanjiv Sarin. His keen eye for every detail and immense patience ensured an amazing final product that you are holding in your hands.

I take pride in extending my heartfelt thanks to Ms Sapna Chauhan, Vice Chairperson Amiown (Amity's Caring Preschools) and ACERT (Amity Centre for Educational Research and Training), to have given me a wonderful platform for nine long years, from 2007 to 2016, as a Teacher-Trainer at ACERT and Parent Counsellor at Amiown, where I could interact with teachers and parents through my ongoing trainings and workshops. Often, the teachers reported that what they had learned at these workshops and trainings, when they actually applied it in their personal and professional lives, they could achieve success. This was very inspiring and motivating and encouraged me to write this book. Whatever has been written in this book has been tried and tested and has been experienced by many. I want to extend my special thanks to all the respected members of the Amity Management who have always wholeheartedly supported my work and my journey as an author.

My sincere thanks to all the teachers I have interacted with till now. My heartfelt thanks to all my students at ACERT and all my Amiown teachers, who have been very receptive to my teachings and my strategies. They have been using them in their journey and have been sharing their victories with me.

I also want to thank all the people who spared their precious time to give the testimonials, which I value very much.

My heartfelt thanks to my two friends, Sunita and Deepti, who have always been enthusiastic about my ventures and have always encouraged me in my writing. I am truly blessed to have them in my life.

My family is my source of unconditional love and support, which energizes me every moment. Thank you, Rajeev, Chirag, and Roshan, for always being there for me and for always appreciating my work and keeping me intrinsically and extrinsically motivated so that I could create my third book. Maddy, my bundle of joy, thanks for being my best buddy, always by my side even when I was writing in the middle of the night. Thanks Mom, Dad, and my brother for your blessings, always. And thank you, God, for your supreme blessings all along this journey.

I have loved every moment in the making of this book and I am sure you will love reading it, too.

Preface

Let Me Make a Difference, Mom & Dad is a comprehensive guide for each and every teacher for meaningfully contributing in the making of a child's personality. This book is a ready reckoner and a crash course for every individual who embarks on this beautiful journey of becoming a teacher. And I can assure you, dear readers, that every time you pick up this book to read, you'll have a new takeaway which will enrich you as a teacher.

During my professional journey of 25 years of teaching, learning and evolving, I have had the privilege of interacting with teachers from all across India. I have been associated with this profession by virtue of imparting trainings to teachers on a wide range of topics related to their profession. During these interactions, I felt that there were a lot of missing links. I could also see many blinkers which were blocking their vision and perception. Though I continued to make efforts to remove these blinkers through my trainings and interactions with the teachers, there was an inner desire to reach out to all teachers in all parts of the country and so this book was conceived. However, it just remained at the idea stage for a long time.

But last year, when my younger son completed his schooling, I felt that the storehouse of my experiential learning was now full enough. So I decided to collate my insights, which I had gained all along, in the form of a book.

The contents of this book have come from my experiential journey as a student, the journey of my children as students, my journey as a teacher and now as a Teacher-Trainer, Parent Counsellor, and an author, and my immediate environment. I have experienced the impact of my teachers on my personality and the impact of my personality on my students. Now, when I counsel and prepare would-be teachers for their journey as teachers, I feel there are enough experiences with me which require to be shared with all.

Let me share two experiences of mine from my school time. I had a teacher who always appreciated my writing. She had unconditional belief in me. And I am a writer today. I also had a teacher who always told me that Maths was not my cup of tea. Even today I shy away from numbers.

My dear friends, when we become teachers, we get a huge amount of magical powers. How we use this power is our choice. But always remember, your magic can either make or break a child's personality and future. So be extremely sensitive and careful how you use your powers. As teachers become aware, become conscious, because you are contributing to the making of the child's personality.

Let Me Make a Difference, Mom & Dad is a must-read for every adult embarking on the journey to become a teacher, teachers who are already in this profession, other educators, Principals and, above all, this book is meant for every Teachers Training Programme all across the country. I am absolutely sure that there will be a takeaway for every teacher who goes through the pages of this book.

Last, but not the least, I want to convey an earnest message to all of you who are thinking of becoming teachers. It's a sincere request and a friendly advice—please do not choose this profession as a stop-gap arrangement, or just to earn some pocket money or because it suits your present arrangement in life. You should join this profession only if you love working with children and are passionate about it. Please remember you are impacting children for life and if you are not happy being with them, it will have an effect on them because more than 90% of communication happens through body language.

Become a teacher by choice and choose to contribute meaningfully in the making of the personality of every child you interact with, because you, my dear teachers, contribute in the making of the characters of the children you teach. You are the Character Educator and have an immense responsibility in the building of the character of this nation.

On this note, I would like to share this beautiful poem with you:

I Am Looking for a Teacher

I am looking for a teacher
Who is beautiful inside
Honest with the students
Giving them a sense of pride

I am looking for a teacher
With a healthy self-esteem
Who clearly states the rules
And doesn't have to scream

I am looking for a teacher
Who creatively prepares
But whose first priority
Is to convey that she cares

I am looking for a teacher
Who is interested, not aloof
Who treats her students with respect
Even when they goof

I am looking for a teacher
Who knows how to laugh and smile
Who enjoys what she's doing
And goes the extra mile
I am looking for a teacher
Who believes all students can learn
Who praises their efforts and talents
When they give their best return

I am looking for a teacher
Who communicates with parents well
Gently and carefully selecting words
When there's a problem to tell

I am looking for a teacher
Who will fill a child with desire
To love to learn more every day
With curiosity that won't tire

I am looking for a teacher
Who encourages children to have a dream
To work at solving problems
Building their self esteem

There are teachers out there
The kind I'm looking for,
For their students' future success
They have opened up the door.

Marilyn Pattison

I really believe that each one of you holding this book in your hands, is this beautiful teacher who will teach and be there for all those children out there waiting enthusiastically for you.

It is with great enthusiasm that I would like to mention three books whose content I found absolutely relevant to my thought process, which I have quoted in this book as well. They are:

You Can Heal Your Life by Louise L. Hay,
Mindset by Dr Carol S. Dweck,
The 7 habits of Highly Effective People by Stephen R. Covey.

The Bibliography at the end has two motives. First and foremost, it is to thank all the writers whose books I have studied and learnt from as a Teacher-Trainer and Parent Counsellor. The second purpose, of course, is to offer you a list of suggestive reads so that you can maximize upon your learning.

Wishing you abundant joy and infinite happiness in this magnificent journey of yours as a teacher!

Dr Bindu Selot
Author, Teacher-Trainer, and Parent Counsellor

www.drbinduselot.com
www.facebook.com/drbinduselot
www.twitter.com/drbinduselot
mail@drbinduselot.com

Contents

	Acknowledgements	13
	Preface	15
1.	Let Me Reinvent Myself	21
2.	I Need to Practise a Growth Mindset	43
3.	Let Me Be the Correct Role Model	51
4.	I Need to Check Out My Burnout State	55
5.	Let Me Sharpen My Skills	61
6.	I Need to Communicate to Relate	67
7.	Let Me Follow My Intuition	77
8.	I Need to Teach to Reach	83
9.	Let Me Be a Story Teller	89
10.	I Need to Be a Thorough Professional	95
11.	Let Me Practise Affirmations	101
	Bibliography	110

1

Let Me Reinvent Myself

It's never too late to reinvent yourself.

Darlene Quinn

During this journey of mine, I have often observed that all of us, including me, have been conditioned to change others, which, unknowingly, just happens to us by way of our nature and nurture. We constantly comment on how others behave, we discuss and dissect their weaknesses, give them unwanted suggestions, and try to influence them to follow our way of working and thinking.

But how many of us are actually aware of our own selves? Who am I? What is my aim in life? What are my strengths? What are my weaknesses? Until and unless we are aware about our own selves, how can we be effective human beings and, above all, effective teachers?

During my regular interactions with teachers, I ask them to give answers to questions like: Who am I? What am I good at? What are the areas that I need to work upon? What is my purpose in life? Where do I want to be five years from now? They are unable to write even a line or two to answer these questions.

Once I asked these questions from a group of trainee teachers. After they completed this file on themselves, they said that this was the first time they had ever thought about themselves. When they wrote about their strengths, their goals, and their thoughts, most of them felt great. After doing this exercise, they confessed that they had rediscovered themselves as individuals.

Now that they knew so much about themselves, they were more ready to work upon themselves because there is only one thing that we have a complete command and control upon, and that is our own self. Unknowingly, instead of working upon ourselves, we spend our entire life working on others.

At this juncture, I want to share this beautiful composition with you, which I often use in my lectures in my class.

> ## I Wanted to Change the World
>
> When I was a young man, I wanted to change the world. I found it was difficult to change the world, so I tried to change my nation.
>
> When I found I couldn't change the nation, I began to focus on my town. I couldn't change the town and as an older man, I tried to change my family.
>
> Now, as an old man, I realize the only thing I can change is myself, and suddenly I realize that if long ago I had changed myself, I could have made an impact on my family. My family and I could have made an impact on our town. Their impact could have changed the nation and I could indeed have changed the world.
>
> **Author: Unknown Monk, 1100 A.D.**

So, dear teachers, when you choose this profession, you are definitely going to make a difference, but whether it will be positive or negative is completely in your hands. I, therefore, take the liberty of asking you a question:

Are you in this profession by choice?

Or

Is it some kind of an arrangement that forced you to become a teacher and you are here by chance?

It will be great to think of following some other profession if you are here by chance, because if you are not passionate about teaching, then you are at the wrong place. You cannot and should not have a casual approach in this profession of teaching to build children and their future.

The first step towards becoming an effective teacher is by reinventing ourselves. This can only be achieved when we become aware of ourselves, develop a relation with ourselves and, above all, love ourselves unconditionally and are ready to embark upon a lifelong journey of working on ourselves.

In spite of being in this beautiful profession of learning and teaching for the last 25 years, being a Teacher-Trainer, a Parent Counsellor, and an author, I am still engaged in the practice of working on myself. Without fail, I invest a minimum of two hours every day to work on my mental, emotional, and physical health, which can only be possible when I am aware about myself.

A Self Awareness Checklist for Teachers

1. How is my overall health?

In order to be a positively impactful teacher, the most important thing is to take care of your health first. Usually, we are very conscious about our physical health, we eat healthy food, and exercise our bodies. But from now onwards, when we mention taking care of health, we refer to the three most important areas of your health:

a. Physical health
b. Emotional health
c. Mental health

Therefore, if we want to be successful personally and professionally, we have to take good, rather great, and daily care of ourselves. You, dear teachers, are the vertebral columns of your families and the society, so taking care of yourself is important if you love your family, your country, and the children, as you would be impacting them for life.

For *physical health*, take nutritious diet, and exercise, daily. My experience in this regard is that each one of us is a different individual, so we need to know our body and take care of it accordingly. Some of the magic mantras that I have used and which are very effective are:

1. Take at least 4 to 5 litres of water every day.
2. Take small meals at regular intervals. Typically, for a full day role of a teacher, you should have at least two meals during the working hours.
3. Plan a healthy breakfast, and a heavy one too, which will provide you the energy required for the day full of action.
4. Try and make sure that you have your meals on time.
5. Do not have tea or coffee on an empty stomach. They are diuretic and acidic in nature. Having them on an empty stomach will make you very uncomfortable during the day.
6. Exercise daily. Choose any form of exercise that you are fond of. It could be yoga, walking, gymming, swimming, dancing, and so on, but without fail invest one hour in this activity every day. This activity will keep you positive and healthy and will increase your immunity as well.
7. Try and consume one lemon each day. You can add it to the water you are drinking or take it in any other form. Lemon has a highly alkaline effect and will help you maintain the pH balance of your body.

For *emotional health*, work on your emotional quotient or EQ, that is, how to handle people and situations. The way you keep an eye on the children in your class, keep a check on your TEA system (T= Thoughts, E=Emotions, A=Actions) in the same way.

If you can handle and make a change at the thought level, the job will be done. You will not have to work on your emotions because they will automatically be taken care of and so would be your actions.

When you are interacting with people, if there are positive transactions taking place, it is fine, but if somebody is sending negative vibrations to you and saying things which hurt you, you have three options. The first one is the regular tit-for-tat, that is, give it back to them. Many a times we cannot do so, so the second option is to absorb the hurt or the negative vibration and keep it with us, which, over time, becomes resentment. However, we have a beautiful third option which is known as *transforming the energy* according to Sister Shivani of Brahmakumari fame. This means that, in spite of the fact that someone is saying hurtful things to you, you have the power to transform the energy exchange by sending them positive vibrations of peace and purity. Try it out. It really works. I have been in this practice for long now and the results are amazing.

For *mental health*, you will have to read or listen daily to something empowering and positive. Just as food is to the body, reading or listening is to the mind. Filter everything before it enters your mind. Violence and negative news, which you see on TV, has a disturbing impact on all of us. Remember, you have the greatest of all powers, and that is the power to choose. You are always particular about eating a nutritious and balanced meal for the health of your body. Similarly, choose the food for your mind with utmost care because there is no room there at all for junk.

When you are able to take care of all the three areas, you become holistically healthy. Then you will be the best tool for the change which you want to see in others. This quote by Mahatma Gandhi is very appropriate:

Be the change you want to see in the world.

2. How is my TEA system?

There is no shortcut to success. You have to work on yourself constantly. You, my dear friends, are not in competition with others—you are only competing with yourself. Whatever you were yesterday, you have to be a better version today and tomorrow you must be a still better version. This beautiful journey of rediscovery can only begin by becoming aware of your thoughts, that is, constantly working on your TEA system.

This is what Sister Shivani of Brahmakumaris also talks about. This is what the book *The Secret* by Rhonda Byrne is based upon. This means it will be great if you could work on choosing the positive thoughts in every situation. Based on that, your emotions get generated. Your emotions drive your actions. So, dear teachers, when you choose your thoughts consciously, you are actually taking care of your actions, which is what behaviour is.

So let's work on our TEA system constantly and become conscious of ourselves.

3. Early morning programing

Program your mind first thing in the morning after you get up. The first 10 minutes are the most precious for the rest of the day. Thanks to Louise L. Hay, and thanks to Sister Shivani, this practice of mine has been my energy tonic for the day. It works wonders. The only thing is that you will have to practise this regularly in order to see the difference in a short time frame. When you get up in the morning your mind is very fertile and it is the quality of thoughts that you sow at that time which will determine how your day will be.

It has been years since I got liberated from my habit of reading the newspaper first thing in the morning. I now go through my newspaper only in the evening. In the morning, when I get up, I thank God, I thank all the parts of my body. I talk to myself and say, "Today is a beautiful day and I can make a difference." Then I stand in front of the mirror and program my mind for the day. I say a smiling "Hello" to myself. I tell myself that I love myself. I talk to myself and say all the good things that I validate about myself, for example,

"You are a great mother, a great wife, a great teacher, a great daughter, a great author, a great employer, etc." Then I say to myself, "I know challenges will be there during the day, but I know you can handle them all. Have a great day ahead!" Finally, I give a thumbs up to myself. This is what marks the beginning of my day.

This talk in front of the mirror to myself has become such a ritual that I can't think of missing it even for a single day. And in spite of all the challenges, my day is smooth because I had programed it early in the morning.

All the people who apply this method can soon see a major difference in their lives. Thoughts have power and when you sow the right, healthy, and positive thoughts in your mind, they take care of everything else.

4. How healthy is my self-esteem?

Another aspect of self-awareness and reinventing yourself is knowing about what all are you capable of or are good at. So, dear teachers, make a list of all your strengths and also a list of all your concerns. Make posters of your strengths and put them around in your room to remind you that you are capable of so much. Make goals to overcome your concerns and take the required actions. Remember that the first step is the most difficult. Once you take the first step, there will be no looking back.

Safeguard your self-esteem. Everyone is born with a very healthy self-esteem, but it is unfortunate that, over a period of time, our self-esteem starts getting diseased and sick, and starts diminishing. This is because we let any Tom, Dick, and Harry deposit opinions about us in our minds. We let them label us and pass judgments. Then we absorb all of that and make this our inner voice, a voice which is always repeating that we are not good enough. When this message plays over and over again, our self-esteem starts getting eroded. With the passage of time, we become mentally, emotionally, and physically weak.

Also, whenever you accomplish a task, validate yourself by appreciating your own self. Be proud about it, rather than always expecting validation from others around, because when you do that you give the remote control of your happiness to others. What is actually required is to take your emotional remote control in your hands, because it's all about you and your life.

5. How is my Resilience Quotient?

Resilience quotient, RQ, is the ability to bounce back from setbacks, tragedies, and failures that each one of us encounters during this life's journey.

Life is not a bed of roses for anybody. There will be ups and downs, happiness and sorrow, celebrations and tragedies. What is important is our ability to bounce back even after major setbacks. This is resilience.

Research says that resilience is a skill that can be taught. Before getting to teach it, we have to first practise resilience.

I would like to narrate a real story here.

> I met this very smart, confident, and positive young lady six years ago at my friend's place. She was actually interested in taking a counselling session related to her son's behavioural issues. The appointment was fixed and she came for the session. During the session when I had a detailed interaction with her, I came to know that she had lost her husband in a fatal accident a year ago. And now she was the only earning member in her family, which included her mother and a younger sister, who was doing her graduation. In another shocking revelation, she also shared the irreparable loss of her only brother, who was five years younger to her. Both the tragedies had occurred within a span of 6 months.

> Her child had got deeply impacted by these incidents and had become withdrawn. She was really concerned about him and wanted to know how she could help him become his cheerful self once again.
>
> After the entire discussion, I gave her the required strategies. Towards the end of the session, when she was about to leave the room, she said that she was very happy because she could now walk confidently on her own. She said that in the accident where she had lost her husband, the lower portion of her left leg was crushed badly, and had to be amputated. She had been worried that she would not be able to walk. But now, with the prosthesis in place, she felt independent and confident.
>
> She was very gracious, happy, and confident, with a very high self-esteem. When she walked out of the room, she taught me one of the most important lessons of life, that is, bouncing back.

Resilience is an attitude, resilience is a skill. The more you practise it, the better it becomes. So let's start practising the skill of bouncing back after each setback and make resilience our attitude. Because we are the role models for them, by practising resilience, we will be teaching one of the most important life skills to our children and loved ones.

6. How are my stress levels?

I have often heard teachers say, day in and day out, "Today, I am really stressed out." And when you repeat something daily, it becomes your inner voice.

We have also learnt that stress is a part of everybody's daily life and that we do not have any control on it because it happens due to factors which are out of our control. External situations and other people are responsible for our stress, so we give the remote control of managing our stress to the external factors.

Actually, stress is an inside affair, wherein we have the power to choose. Let me share this hypothetical situation with you:

One day, all of you were called to the Principal's office, where she gave you a good and strong lecture for not staying back after school to complete your tasks for the Annual Day function, due to which there was chaos and confusion in the morning and the function could not start on time. Now suppose there are five of you—one of you might be upset for a minute, one for 5 minutes, one for 10 minutes, one for a day, and the last one might be upset because of this for 10 days.

So, in spite of everybody getting the same stimulus, the response was different. Each of us has different abilities to accommodate, understand, and absorb the learning and then finish and delete the memory and move ahead.

From today onwards, let's change our understanding of stress—*we* are the ones who have the remote control to manage our stress by choosing to hold or not to hold on to it. Instead of holding on, let us learn, delete and move on from every experience and situation.

If we are going to hold on to stress for long, it will cause physical, mental, and emotional ailments. And, dear teachers, words have great power. Let's enjoy the beautiful journey of being a teacher and never use words like "I am stressed out today." Instead, saying "I am enjoying my day today" will have a very positive impact on your overall health.

Here is a beautiful story on stress, which is very close to my heart. I often use it in my lectures.

The carpenter I hired to help me restore an old farmhouse had just finished a rough first day on the job. A flat tyre made him lose an hour of work, his electric saw quit, and then his ancient pick-up truck refused to start.

While I drove him home, he sat in stony silence. On arriving, he invited me in to meet the family. As we walked towards the front door, he paused briefly at a small tree, touching the tips of the branches with both hands.

After opening the door, he underwent an amazing transformation. His face was wreathed in smiles, and he hugged his two small children and then gave his wife a kiss. Afterwards, he walked me to my car. We passed the tree, and my curiosity got the better of me. I asked him about what I had seen him do earlier.

"Oh, that's my worry tree," he replied. "I know I can't help having worries on the job, but one thing I know for sure, worries don't belong to my house where I stay with my wife and children. So I just hang them upon the tree every night when I come home. Then, in the morning, I pick them up again."

"Funny thing is," he smiled, "when I come out in the morning to pick them up, there aren't nearly as many as I remember hanging up the night before."

Unknown author

So, dear teachers, even you can hang your stress and worries on your worry tree or write them down on post-its and post them on your stress and worry absorbing tree before you sleep. The next morning you are sure to find many stresses and worries just vanishing. I have tried this technique on myself and it really works.

Another way of understanding this is by an example. Raise your hand and hold a one-litre bottle of water in your hand. Do you know what will happen to your muscles? They will start aching. After some time, probably 10 minutes or so, you will not be able to hold the bottle any more. In this situation, you will simply keep the bottle down. This is exactly what you need to do when you are stressed. You are not supposed to hold your stress for long. Instead, either keep it down or hang it before you sleep and see the miracle unfold. Because now, you have the remote control of stress in your hands.

From now on, understand what STRESS should stand for:

S=Stop

T=Turn to your thoughts

R=Remember to be positive

E=Erase all negativity

S=Smile to yourself

S=Start again

7. Where is my focus: on the problem or on the solution?

So far, we have seen that we have the power to choose from the variety of situations life has to offer us. Let us check, in a typical day, whether our focus is on problems or on solutions. You can do this small exercise and you will come to know your situation.

> Close your eyes for a minute and experience what happens to you. There can be different things that can happen to different persons. Some will start counting time and are eager for the one minute to be over so that they can open their eyes; some will be busy trying to listen to their surroundings; some will be revisiting their day; and for some it will be a relaxation time.

This is an exercise to help you understand where your focus is. All those waiting for that one minute to be over were concentrating on the problem. All others who lost the track of the time and were creatively engaged were concentrating on solutions that they had opted for during that one minute.

In this manner, in our life, we will always have two situations—a problem and a solution. If we focus on the problem, we are caught and entangled in a tricky situation. But if we focus on the solution instead of the problem, we will be making our lives much easier.

Here is another exercise to help you understand this concept.

Let's try some opposites:

Black–white

Fat–thin

Day–night

Tall–short

Now let's put our on creative caps and think creatively for more options for opposites:

Black—yellow, orange, green, pink

Fat—lean, tall, slim

Day—dusk, dawn, twilight

Tall—dwarf, bonsai, miniature

When we get a little creative and think out of the box, we will get our solutions. Like we just saw, there can be many opposites. Why were we stuck with only one opposite until now? I can assure you, dear teachers, that the moment you change your focus from the problem to the solution, you will automatically start getting solutions to your problems, because a problem cannot exist without a solution. The fact that *every problem has a solution* should become your new belief.

8. How is my "me" time?

You are wonderful teachers. You have been working so hard managing everybody at home and at school, but do you ever spend time with yourself? Check the status of your "me" time. This is the time which you spend with yourself, doing what you want or like to do, which could be your favourite time. So, if you love listening to songs, if you love painting, if you love watching movies, or just hanging around with friends, just go and do it. Cook or order your favourite dish, just for yourself. Above all, learn to love yourself unconditionally.

You too, my dear teachers, are normal human beings. So what if you have made mistakes? Just be kind and forgive yourself. Guilt, resentment, fear, and anxiety, are all your energy wasters, so nip them in the bud itself.

In order to be able to take care of all around us, we have to invest time in ourselves for our "me" time activities. These could be a hobby or anything that you love doing. Whenever you have done something good, give yourself a gift, take yourself out for a date and pamper yourself. Believe me, you truly deserve this because you are making a difference to the lives of so many.

9. Am I suffering from the "to please" disease?

It is extremely important to be honest to ourselves. As children, we are taught that if we study, mummy will be happy, if we get good marks daddy will be happy and if we don't talk in the class, the teacher will be happy. That is how, unknowingly, our mind gets programed and we start accomplishing tasks to please all the significant adults around us.

Often these tasks become a pressure and a burden. For example, the study course needs to be finished or the correction of books needs to be finished. This is fine and an integral part of a teacher's duty. However, if we do all of this just to please a senior person, then the whole process becomes painful. But if we start pleasing ourselves by reprograming ourselves and taking responsibility, for example, "I am going to finish the course because I am responsible" and "I am going to finish the corrections well in time because it is my duty," then we will not find the process painful.

It is extremely important to enjoy what you are doing because you are here by choice and not by chance. So resist the desire to please others. Instead, please yourself. And if you are not comfortable doing something, have the courage to say "No" politely.

You, therefore, need to be intrinsically motivated. Extrinsic motivation will not be of much help in the long run, because after a certain amount of time, the charm will dwindle. Similarly, on your personal front, if a friend suddenly calls you in the afternoon and wants to drop their child at your place because they have to go somewhere, don't get pushed into saying a "Yes" if you are not comfortable. Afternoon may be your rest and sleep time. Be honest to yourself, share your feelings with your friend and say a logical "No" instead of letting them drop the child and then getting frustrated and feeling suffocated because you were not able to say a "No" as you felt that your friend might feel hurt. Also, let me tell you, all your negative vibrations are sure to reach your friend and complicate the situation. Instead, validate your feelings.

You will have to act on this to be able to experience how important it is to stop pleasing others. Instead, love yourself, value yourself, and start pleasing your own self, to be able to make that difference to the children you teach.

10. How open am I to feedback?

A big and bold fact is that no communication is ever complete without feedback. Unfortunately, most of the time we practise incomplete communication because that is how the environment has conditioned us. Now that we have embarked on this beautiful journey of becoming a teacher, we need to do a reality check to see how open we are to feedback.

Starting from our childhood, we get feedback from the people and the environment around us. How much of it actually gets registered in our system is a great question mark. This happens because everything is dependent on how open we are to feedback.

It is a general human behaviour that feedback which come to us as a compliment is readily accepted by our system, but all the critical feedback often bounces back because, unfortunately, we are not in the habit of accepting such feedback. The fact is that the most critical sounding feedback is the one which, if incorporated in our systems, will do wonders for our overall evolution and growth as a teacher or a human being.

I would like to mention here the famous Johari window, which I have found very useful in understanding my own self. It will be one of the best tools for you, too, to understand yourself. The Johari window is an analysis is used to help people better understand their relationship with themselves and others. It was created by psychologists Joseph Luft (1916-2014) and Harrington Ingham (1916-1995) in 1955.

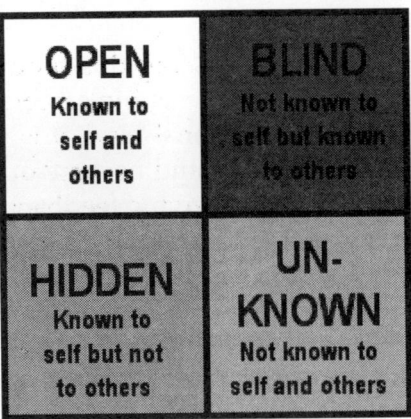

The Johari window model is an extremely effective and fascinating tool to understand ourselves and others.

As you can see, there are four windows to everybody's personality.

The first one is your *Open Window*. This is that part of your personality which is known to you and known to others as well. For example, I am an author. This is known to me and known to you, so this is a part of my open window.

The second one is your *Blind Window*. This is that part of your personality which others around know, but you are unaware about it. An example could be that you are not good at listening to others. All others know this about you, but you do not know this about your own self.

The third one is your *Hidden Window*. This is that part of your personality which only you know of. It is a fact that there are definitely some secrets which each one of us have which we only keep to ourselves, so that this is only known to us and not known to others.

The fourth one is your *Unknown Window*. This is that aspect of your personality which you get to discover only when a totally new situation crops up. Otherwise, neither is it known to you, nor is it known to others. For example, if there is an earthquake right now, neither you know how you would behave in such a situation nor others know how you would behave.

The reason we are discussing this model is that if we want to be successful in our teaching careers and evolve as individuals even in our personal lives, it is very important that we remove our blinkers and become open to feedback from others. If others are not giving feedback, please ask for it. That is the only way to reduce your blind window. As you work towards reducing your blind window by being open to feedback, you automatically increase your open window, which is the window responsible for your evolution.

Here, I cannot stop myself from sharing my example. Since my childhood days, I was regularly getting feedback that I was a chatterbox. I would never let anyone speak, because I would never listen to anybody. Constantly talking was my second nature. Though feedback was repeatedly given by teachers, friends, and parents, but because it was critical, I would brush it aside. I would tell myself, "Why should I bother about how others feel about me? I am perfect the way I am." That resulted in my unknowingly getting into the habit of speaking 80% of the time and listening only 20% of the time.

This habit of mine went on for a long time. Only when I got married and removed my blinkers, did this constant feedback from my husband and my parents become effective, because I was now open to this critical feedback. Because I accepted this feedback, I wanted to work upon it.

This one thing changed my life. I worked so hard on myself that, today, I am a counsellor and I listen 80% of the time and speak for only 20%. I save so much of my energy. I have also developed empathetic listening, which is my best tool, due to which I get so much more insight into my profession and the environment around me.

This experience has contributed in a major way to my personal and professional success.

I am sure that you, dear teachers, will become more open to critical feedback and will always ask for feedback in every communication to make it complete.

11. Am I a reflective, evolutionary practitioner?

No one can claim to be an effective teacher without practising being a reflective, evolutionary practitioner. This means that at the end of every day, you need to review the entire day and try to see how the day progressed, how your approach in the class while giving the concepts was, could you achieve your goals, could you involve the students, could learning happen, and so on. Based on your reflections, you evolve with each passing day by doing away with something which did not work and by adding something new that worked.

When I say that each and every teacher across the entire globe needs to practise being a reflective, evolutionary practitioner, I say it because reflections are an integral part of daily teaching and learning process. Just to practise reflections will be of no use if you do not evolve your approach, your lesson plans, your contingency plans, your methods of handling children and their behaviour, based on your daily reflections.

Teaching, learning, and evolving is an ongoing process. It must go on till we are teaching and growing. This is how nature also works. The flightless birds and the dinosaurs of the past could not evolve, so they had to become extinct. Similarly, in teaching you will get the same results if you go on following the same style of teaching, unmindfully doing the same things.

So, my dear teachers, ask yourselves often, "Am I a reflective, evolutionary practitioner?" If your answer is "Yes," then try to look for examples from your daily practise of teaching and learning which support your belief. No matter whether you are a preschool teacher or a 12th class teacher, you have to practise this skill of becoming a reflective, evolutionary practitioner.

I recently experienced this in one of the classes. The class teacher came to me with a concern that she was facing a huge challenge of not being able to handle 4-5 children of her class. Whenever she was trying to explain a concept, these 4-5 children were always moving about,

> jumping, pushing, and hitting one another. Due to this, the other children in the class could not concentrate. When she tried to take care of these 4-5 children, the other children became out of control. The whole class became chaotic and she was unable to reach her expected goal for the day.

I sat with the teacher to understand her concern. I observed these children and then gave her the inputs, based on my observations.

I could see that during the classes there were only passive activities, one after the other, which means that the children were either listening to a story, or doing rhymes or getting exposed to a concept while just sitting at their desks. There was hardly any movement in the class. So I suggested that she needed to plan the activities for her class in such a way that there should be alternate active and passive activities. That is, if children listened to a story narration, then after that there should be some activity requiring movement like rhymes, etc. I also told her that she needed to explain each concept in three different ways so that the children with any of the three leaning styles could be engaged.

I am glad to report that this teacher started applying these strategies after reflection. During the narration of a story, she used YouTube links, and then told the students to act out the concept. She would always involve a lot of movement in her concepts and give concrete experiences, which kept these 4-5 children engaged meaningfully. Thus she overcame her challenge effectively.

2

I Need to Practise a Growth Mindset

No matter what your current ability is, effort is what ignites that ability and turns it into accomplishment.

Carol S. Dweck

Since the time I came across this beautiful book, *Mindset*, by Dr Carol S. Dweck, I simply cannot stop talking about it and its relevance in today's set up. Dr Carol Dweck, with her decades of research, has truly discovered a groundbreaking idea for achieving success in life and that is the power of our mindset. She says that it is not just our abilities and talent that bring us success. The mindset with which we approach our goals plays a major role in how successful we are.

I feel mindset is an extremely important aspect of a teacher's personality. How she interacts with her children and how she encourages and motivates them, will have an impact on them for life.

Therefore, if you want to be an effective, impactful teacher, then you necessarily have to get out of your fixed mindset and embrace the growth mindset.

According to Dr Dweck, often teachers praise students to motivate them and to encourage them, with an aim to build their self-esteem. In this process, we might be unknowingly encouraging them to develop a fixed mindset, which might limit their learning potential. However, if we praise students not for what they are but for the process that they have gone through, that is, their hard work, perseverance, commitment, etc., then we, as teachers, are helping them to maximize their potential through a growth mindset that we have established in them.

When students are in a fixed mindset state, they believe that their intelligence, talents, and other abilities are inborn and fixed, so they can't do much about it. Therefore, the challenge for them is how to always look smart and how to present their abilities in a better manner. But when the students are in the growth mindset state, they believe that their intelligence, talents, and other abilities can be developed through genuine efforts, hard work, and perseverance. Thus, we see that the mindset has a great impact in shaping an individual's personality and is based upon their understanding of success and failure.

Fixed mindset people dread failure, because they feel that if they try something and fail at it, then it would reflect imperfectly on their personality; growth mindset people embrace failure as an opportunity to learn, grow and evolve.

Since children have two major pillars, the parents, and the teachers—the two significant sets of adults who impact them for life—it is the moral responsibility of teachers to not just teach academic subjects, but also make sure they help the children develop a growth mindset rather than a fixed mindset.

To be able to become a growth mindset role model, the teachers themselves will have to unlearn their fixed mindset approach and make space to adapt to the new psychology of success—the growth mindset.

I have worked on this myself and I can assure you, dear teachers, that it takes just 21 days to form a new habit. When you are convinced with the logic, you make genuine efforts and smoothly adapt to become a growth mindset teacher. This is the best thing that can happen to any teacher. I am thankful to Dr Carol S. Dweck for sharing this wonderful tool with us.

I have mentioned some strategies which will help you to propel yourself to become a growth mindset teacher, which will be very helpful to you in your personal and professional lives.

Strategies for you to become a growth mindset teacher

1. Always be proud of your growth mindset attitude. As a growth mindset teacher, you must believe that school is not only a platform for students' learning but is also a platform for teachers' learning. So nurture love for learning and use your teaching profession to grow yourself, to remain well informed and equipped with the latest advancements. Never ever think that you know it all. Instead, always be ready to learn and say, "I can learn all the time." You have to improve a little every day to become better than the day before.
2. Accept and acknowledge your true self, which means accept all your concerns as well as your strengths. Shying away from your concerns will not help you. Instead, accepting them will help you to face them and work upon them.
3. Always embrace challenges as opportunities for new learning and growth.
4. Delete the words failure, failing, and mistake from your vocabulary. Actually, that which was called as failing or as a mistake is neither of them. What all you learnt from that attempt is important. So when you couldn't reach your goal, you don't fail but you learn.
5. Stop seeking always the approval of authority figures around you. When you do so, you prioritize approval over learning. In the process, you sacrifice your potential for growth.
6. Always value the process and not the end product. Don't be in a rush to produce the end product. Enjoy the learning process associated with that activity.
7. Always believe that critical feedback needs to be open heartedly accepted by you for your overall growth and development.

8. Take out time every day for reflection. At the end of the day, it would be a great idea to revisit the day and see what worked well and what could have been done a little better.
9. The brain is a muscle, so a regular workout is essential. This means that reading, creating, imagining, brainstorming, and practising divergent thinking are all a must.
10. Always look for solutions instead of focussing on problems. A problem cannot exist without a solution.
11. Embrace change, be proactive, do not get addicted to a comfort zone and complacency. Instead, keep taking new risks.
12. Above all, have a clear sense of purpose of who you are, what you want to be and where you want to reach in life.

Strategies to inculcate growth mindset in your students

1. Growth mindset teachers believe in the growth of the intellect and talent, and they are fascinated with the process of learning. So as a teacher, always validate the process, not the end product. For example, if a child has scored full marks in a test, rather than saying, "Keep it up, you have topped the class and I am proud of you," it would be more appropriate to say, "I really admire the efforts that you put in to prepare for your test. I am proud of your hard work and you, too, should be proud of your efforts and hard work." Always praise the process when interacting with children.
2. Help the students of your class believe that they are happy, powerful learners, and learning is fun.
3. Embrace mistakes, failures, and wrong answers. Fixed mindset teachers do not let students make mistakes or put up questions. Remember, dear teachers, ridicule, and

humiliation will never foster learning. Motivate students through respect, not through fear.

For example, when a student gives a wrong answer, instead of saying, "No, that is a wrong answer," it would be more appropriate to say, "This is not yet the correct answer, but keep it up! Because you tried answering that, I admire your proactiveness and effort. Be proud of yourself for making the effort to answer the question." The takeaway for this child should be that taking risks, participating, and making mistakes are not only OK, but they are positive and important ingredients for achieving success.

4. Break the myth that talent, intelligence, and abilities are inborn and defined at birth. As a growth mindset teacher, always encourage and instil in your students that talent, intelligence, and abilities can all be developed with constant effort, hard work, right motivation, and a nurturing environment. Always begin your class with stories to sensitize them that it is OK to be imperfect and still succeed and it is OK to be you. Show them that perfection is impossible. Narrate to them stories of individuals who overcame obstacles and labels to develop into extraordinary and successful individuals.

5. Collaborate with your students in the process of learning and growth. As a growth mindset teacher, never form preconceived notions about your students. Do not let the teachers who have taught them in the past colour your opinions with their labels. Instead, see the children as fresh learners, with unlimited potential, ready to embark on a new journey with you.

As a growth mindset teacher, on the first day of the class, tell them that we will be collaborators in this partnership of learning, and growth. Tell them that you will support and help them and they need to support and help you. Tell them that in your class they can be who they want to become, not who they were in their previous classes. Tell them that each of them has the skills and capabilities to design their future on their own terms and that the process starts now. Tell them that they are not the products of the past and their futures are not predetermined.

Together, sign a collaborative document for each child. For each one of them, write that they are unique and that you have complete faith and belief in them. Then ask each child to write for themselves what they love about themselves and that they completely believe that with hard work, constant efforts and perseverance, they will fulfil all their dreams for that academic year.

6. Make "Yet" your new magic word whenever you are interacting with students. Whenever a student is struggling with a task tell him or her that they haven't mastered it "Yet" but with a little more effort they will master it for sure.
7. Whenever you are designing activities, as a part of your lesson plan, do it in a manner that you encourage collaborative working rather than competitive working or individual working. Research shows that students are more motivated and successful when they work as a team, collaboratively in groups.
8. Genius is defined by hard work. Tell them that genius is one who works hard, consistently, towards his or her goal and does not only depend on talent and abilities. Give the message to the students that each of them is a developing person and that you, their teacher, are interested in their development.
9. As a teacher, always remember that lowering standards does not raise the self-esteem of children. Neither would raising standards do any wonders. So set high standards of expectations for your children and have your children reach them by helping, supporting and handholding them.

10. When children have messed up, do not give feedback that simply labels or excuses the child. Instead, give constructive, critical feedback which will help them see a clear picture and show them how to deal with the situation and work upon it.
11. As a growth mindset teacher, you need to have unconditional love, deep affection and personal commitment to each student. You have to teach them to live and celebrate the process of learning. Students need to know from you that school is place for them to grow and learn and not fear and withdraw.
12. Talk to your students about your own journey. Talk about your failures, your disappointments and your struggles so that they know you and can relate with you more deeply. Let them know what were the challenges that you faced, the mistakes that you made, the difficult decisions that you took, your failures, and your successes. Research validates that these personal stories of yours have an impact on the mind of the child for life and they will be learning the most important lessons of life through them. So, as a teacher, make your personal stories an integral part of your lesson plan to make that beautiful difference to the lives of your students.

3

Let Me Be the Correct Role Model

Children learn more from what you are than what you teach.

W. E. B. Du Bois

We have often heard that parents are the first teachers of children, but the next most impactful persons are the teachers who teach them at school.

Once you join the teaching fraternity, it is extremely important that you understand the impact of your words. Whether you encourage a child or you discourage a child, both have equal impact on the psyche of the child and play a major role in shaping their personality.

I would like to share my own example.

When I was a child, studying in the sixth standard, I was often told by my Maths teacher that Maths was not my cup of tea. He said that I was not cut out for Maths so often that Maths became my ugly frog. I would like to confess here today that I was scared of anything to do with numbers. This label became the programing of my subconscious mind and I left Maths after tenth standard. I could only face this fear of mine when, unknowingly, my anxiety, and avoidance of Maths started impacting my children. I decided to face my fear and overcome it. When I faced Maths and revisited my experiences, I found that Maths was the basis of everything around me. It was not Maths that I feared but I feared my Maths teacher at school. So I disassociated the two and when I had no fear, Maths looked very interesting and simple. I changed my programing for Maths so as to make sure that I did not pass on this anxiety to my children and I was successful.

Let Me Be the Correct Role Model

I will share another experience of mine.

> When I was in second standard, I had the most empathetic teacher, who was soft spoken, always positive, always very encouraging. She always focussed on a child's positive abilities and strengths. On a daily basis, she would compliment us. She was also my English teacher. We had the second last period as the writing period, where we were supposed to write one page daily in the class and get it checked by her. I am so proud to share that every day I got good, very good, excellent and stars for my writing. Because of her encouraging words and motivation, I love writing till today. In spite of the fact that now we write everything electronically, I still enjoy writing with fountain pens whenever I get a chance. The words of encouragement and the positive validation of my work by my beautiful teacher became the programing of my subconscious mind. Finally, my love for writing helped me explore the unknown and I became a writer. In fact, this is my third book. Such is the impact of the positive labels and such is an impact of negative labels as well.

Recently, I met a child during one of my counselling sessions. We were exploring options after class 12, in spite of the fact that this child's dream was to become a teacher. But because she did not have good experiences with her initial two teachers, she was hesitant to become a teacher.

So, dear teachers, take the moral responsibility of consciously being the correct role models because you impact for life the children you interact with. Remember, based on how you behave in the class, children form an opinion about this profession. So take a pledge that you will make sure that you, through your role model, will present that teaching is one of the most noble and pious professions, where life is full of learning and evolving, every moment.

Through your role model, you need to convey another, most important, thing to children and that is they are developing young individuals and you, as a teacher, are passionately interested in their development.

4

I Need to Check Out My Burnout State

Burnout is not caused by doing too many things. It is likely evidence that there may be too many things you've not been doing.

Ben Kubassek

When we become teachers, we need to keep in mind that each and every action of ours and each and every word of ours has an impact on a child for life. So only when we learn the art of switching on and switching off in terms of our other roles, we actually become a teacher.

While being teachers, we have many other roles as well — as a parent, as a spouse, as a homemaker, and so on. We are always multitasking, which is an essential skill of a teacher. But how many of us have learned to switch on the teacher role and switch off all other roles that we play, once we are in school? Though we have been hearing this many times, but are we able to put this skill into practice? It is extremely important for teachers to gather themselves emotionally, set their emotional tone and then enter the class. Otherwise, before you have actually begun your day, you are already emotionally facing a burnout.

When you enter the class in that state, you are actually damaging the learning and teaching process. In the disturbed state, you may convey demeaning messages to the children, which plays havoc on their self-esteem. The child keeps wondering where he or she went wrong to get that reaction from their teacher.

This is a real incident experienced by my son when he was in class four.

One day, in the afternoon, my son came back home from school, with a long face. He was quiet and not his usual chirpy self. When I asked him how his day was, he did not reply. He just went to his room, dumped his school bag and came out carrying a dictionary. While turning the pages, he asked me, "Mom, do you know what is the meaning of hopeless?" I said, "Yes, it means somebody who is not good enough." Then I questioned him, "But why are you asking me that?" Pat came the reply, "Today my class teacher said in front of the whole class that both the monitors of the class are hopeless." My son was one of the monitors. The teacher had made the statement because they had not written the names of the children who were making noise.

I kept on telling him that it was OK, that the teacher actually did not mean what she said, she was probably just upset that you had not performed your role as a monitor, she actually loves you and cares for you, she always appreciates you whenever I have gone for PTMs or to meet her at other occasions. Even by the evening, my son was feeling very hurt and low and kept on asking me, "Mom, am I not good enough? Why did Ma'am say that I am hopeless? Am I hopeless? What will I do in my life if I am hopeless?"

I happened to have good rapport with his class teacher and I could not stop myself. I called her up and shared this whole experience with her and I told her the impact of what she had said on my son. She was very apologetic. She honestly confessed that she was just in a bad mood because her maid had not turned up that day. She also had a major showdown with her mother-in-law in the morning. That was why she got irritated at every little thing that morning. So she may have said that both the monitors were hopeless, but she did not mean hurt anyone. I made my son talk to her. She counselled him and told him that she did not mean to hurt him.

You can see the large, unintended impact of the emotional outburst of this teacher, who forgot to check her emotional burnout state before going to the class. My question to you, dear teachers, is — Are you checking and taking care of your emotional burnout before entering the class? This is a very important skill which needs to be practised by every teacher on a daily basis before she or he actually enters the class.

Let us make entering a class full of children as the most pious activity. For that we will have to be planning and preparing in advance. So, as a teacher, it is extremely important for you to go for a counselling session once in a while so that you can get timely guidance, take a short break, unwind, and keep yourself emotionally recharged. This is only possible by constantly working upon yourself on all the aspects given in the first chapter of this book.

Valuing yourself, valuing your time, valuing your voice will go a long way in achieving this.

Everybody has an emotional bank from which there are regular withdrawals, but hardly any deposits. Do not keep waiting for others to deposit love, appreciation and validation of your emotions. Instead, learn the art of developing a relation with yourself.

To keep yourself emotionally hydrated, once in a while pamper yourself, take a break, do whatever you have been wanting to do for long. Never be angry with yourself, love yourself unconditionally and, on a daily basis, spend "me" time with yourself. Remember teachers, there is nothing more important than taking care of your emotional self first, so that you don't reach the emotional burnout state.

Keep your emotions in check. The children who you teach are not your emotional pillows, so take care of your repressed emotions. Look for alternate solutions to deal with them. I have come across several cases where the brunt of the emotional burnout of the teacher had to be faced by an innocent child. A very simple start could be, start keeping an account of your emotions. Check your emotions, give them time, deal with them, and then prepare yourself for the class. The way you plan in the morning what dress to wear, in the same way program your mind and wear suitable emotions for the day. You could choose from such a wide range — enthusiastic, happy, energetic, positive, and so on.

So what if you had a bad start of the day — you may be upset because your maid did not come to work, you had to prepare breakfast, you got late, you missed the bus, you had to rush and finally you arrived late on a Monday morning. All of this should not reach the class with you. Remember teachers, you always have two options to choose from, so choose the right one.

In this case itself, you had a choice when your maid called up to say that she could not come for work. You could have two thoughts. The first one, which comes naturally to us, is, "Oh God, maids always ditch you when you require them the most. Even though I gave a new saree on Diwali, she still did this to me. She must be absolutely fine, I am sure. This is simply an excuse made by her."

But if we check ourselves and not let our negative emotions overpower us, then the other thought could be, "OK, she is not well. After all, she is also a human being. She works so hard, she must have fallen ill. We get at least a Sunday off, but maids are working every day for us." In this situation, maybe you will politely talk to her, tell her to take rest and take medicines, hope she gets well soon and then proceed to have a little conversation with yourself about how you will manage the day. You can pack a fruit tiffin, or at school take something from the canteen and once you are back, you may decide to order lunch from outside, and then, in the evening you will manage because you will be home.

When you are in control of your emotions by choosing the right ones, you are calm, composed, and in control of yourself. Then the situations are in your control.

Nothing in life is perfect and difficult situations will come. Don't you handle so many challenges during a typical day as a teacher? Similarly, be conscious, and completely accept a difficult situation. Stop focusing on problems; look for solutions. When you consciously work on implementing this habit, you will be extremely successful.

But do not give up before trying for at least 21 days. This is a tried and tested strategy. For you to learn any habit and unlearn the old one, a minimum period of 21 days is required.

So take charge, take command of the situation, and regularly check your emotional burnout state. Above all, become your own counsellor. When negative emotions start blocking your thought clarity, take a one minute break. If you can reach a mirror, talk to yourself the way you would have talked to a friend to calm them down and help them. Do this and, I promise, you will be back on track.

So, dear teachers, take the emotional remote control in your hand and don't let others around you ever get an access to it.

5

Let Me Sharpen My Skills

Only the people who take learning, growth and skills development into their own hands will be tomorrow's leaders.

Alli Worthington

In his book *7 Habits of Highly Effective People*, Steven Covey has talked about some very important skills. In fact, I found the book very useful for teachers. Here is a beautiful story by him:

> A man was walking through a forest when he came across a frustrated lumberjack.
>
> The lumberjack was trying to cut down a tree with his saw and was swearing and cursing as he laboured in vain.
>
> "What's the problem?" the man asked.
>
> "My saw's blunt and won't cut the tree properly," the lumberjack responded.
>
> "Why don't you just sharpen it?"
>
> "Because then I would have to stop sawing," said the lumberjack.
>
> "But if you sharpened your saw, you could cut more efficiently and effectively than before."
>
> "But I don't have time to stop!" The lumberjack retorted, getting more frustrated.
>
> The man shook his head and kept on walking, leaving the lumberjack to his pointless frustration.

This story is relevant to so many of us, isn't it?

We get frustrated by life and our inability to cope. But instead of developing ourselves and taking the time to become more effective, we keep struggling with a blunt saw.

Don't do this any more. Stop, sharpen your saw and become more effective.

Let Me Sharpen My Skills

"Sharpen the Saw" means preserving and enhancing the greatest asset you have. It means having a balanced programme for self-renewal in the five areas of your life – physical, social, emotional, mental, and spiritual.

I have always loved this quote of Abraham Lincoln:

"Given me six hours to chop down a tree and I will spend the first four sharpening the axe."

During my workshops, I ask teachers to talk and share how much time they spend in sharpening their axe. It is a matter of great concern that teachers cannot relate to this activity. Unfortunately, some don't even have any idea of what we are talking about. A few of them end up saying, "Where is the time? We are always overburdened and are multitasking, so there is no time to sharpen the axe."

To that, my dear teachers, I would say that then there would be very little chance of you being able to evolve, enjoy, and make a difference. You will miss out on maximising your potential and being effective as a teacher. As per Darwin's theory of survival of the fittest, my dear teachers, to be an effective teacher and maintain that status, it is extremely important that you invest a significant part of your time in sharpening your axe on a daily basis, to be able to be a part of this profession.

The activities which will help you to sharpen your axe are:

1. Work on self. Try to become more and more aware about yourself. The most important thing is becoming aware about yourself and then you can start working upon yourself, which cannot stop till you breathe your last.
2. Be proactive and look for opportunities to learn. Take new challenges and come out of your comfort zone.
3. Value yourself. Invest in "me" time with yourself on a daily basis.

4. Use your voice as if you are using money. Speak only when required and listen as much as you can. Develop this skill and you will be amazed how much you can learn every day.
5. Keep checking your TEA system regularly. During the day, check it every hour. If there are negative thoughts, change them.
6. Sister Shivani, of the Brahmakumari fame, says that we produce almost 60,000 thoughts in a day. Research shows that out of these, 80% are related to the past, 15% are related to the future, so for the present we are only left with 5%. She also says that thoughts related to the past and future are wasteful thoughts. So we actually have only 5% useful thoughts. This is a serious issue. We need to consciously reflect upon it and work on it.
6. Always be interested in your professional development. You have to keep updating yourself to be able to cope with the ever evolving education system and the ever evolving children. Whenever there are workshops arranged by your school for you, make their best use. Be enthusiastic, take notes, ask questions, and try to maximize on the opportunity, instead of just waiting for the workshop to finish so that you can go home. When I see a teacher coming for a workshop without a notepad, I know how closed that teacher is for learning. As a teacher, a notepad and a pen is a part of your kit; you should always have it handy.
7. Practise 10 minutes of DEAR time daily. DEAR time means Drop Everything and Read (Reference: *Ramona Quimby, Age 8* by Beverly Cleary). There is no shortcut to reading. No matter how busy you are, reading for at least 10 minutes every day is definitely possible. The way food is for the body, similarly reading is the food for the brain. You cannot afford to starve your brain.

I was so much convinced by this concept that I read out to my sons daily, without fail. Every day we, as a family, had a fixed book reading schedule. The result was that all of us love reading books. Similarly, I have always encouraged my students to get into practicing DEAR time. To begin with, you can pick up a book which interests you and is easy to read. You can then progress to other books.

I have given a list at the end of this chapter for you as a starting point on what to read.

8. Be very open to feedback and if you are not getting it in the normal course, ask for it. Remember, no communication is complete without a feedback.
9. Do not compare yourself with others. Just be in competition with yourself. Review how you were yesterday and how you are today.
10. Above all, become an evolutionary, reflective, practitioner, that is, spend a couple of minutes daily on reflections. At the end of the day, go through the day, and see what went right and what went wrong, and then incorporate the changes the next day.
11. Enrol for short, certificate courses and workshops. The investment is going to be worth it because this is an important investment for self enhancement.

Mentioned here are some of the most important books that I have benefited from during my evolutionary journey. You can also begin this practice of DEAR time by reading my other two books, *Goodbye Mom & Dad, See You in the Afternoon* and *I Have Issues, Mom & Dad*.

1. *You Can Heal Your Life* by Louise L. Hay. This is a book to help you learn how to heal yourself.
2. *Eat That Frog* by Brian Tracy. This is a book on how to handle procrastination.

3. *Change Your Life* by Sneha Mehta. These are inspirational stories from new age healers.
4. *Mindset* by Dr Carol S. Dweck. This is a book on how you can fulfil your potential.
5. *Because Life Is a Gift* by Disha. This book has stories of hope, courage, and perseverance.
6. *Thought for the Day* by Napoleon Hill and Judith Williamson
7. *Mindfulness Pocketbook* by Gill Hasson. This book has little exercises for a calmer life.
8. *Maximize Your Potential through the Power of Your Subconscious Mind to Overcome Fear and Worry* by Dr Joseph Murphy.
9. *The SuperWoman's Guide to Super Fulfillment* by Jaime Kulaga, PhD.
10. *Dissenting Diagnosis* by Dr Arun Gadre and Dr Abhay Shukla. This is an amazing book, worth reading.

A longer list of useful books to read is given in the Bibliography at the end of this book.

6

I Need to Communicate to Relate

Our task is to help children communicate with the
world using all their potential, strength and languages
and to overcome any obstacle presented by
our culture.

Lorris Malaguzzi

Communication is an important skill for every person. Teachers and communication go hand in hand. As you become a teacher, you start communicating meaningfully with three groups. The first group is the parents. You have to communicate regularly with the parents to be able to collaborate with them and to support the learning and growth in the children. The second group is your children and the third group is your peer group as well as your seniors and juniors.

I believe, after all the variety of experiences I have had during this journey of mine, that communication is one of the most important tools in the hands of a teacher. It plays a major role in the success of the teacher. So, dear teachers, always take care that you are not just communicating, but that you are communicating effectively with all the three groups that you interact with on a regular basis.

Effective communication does not mean only giving messages efficiently from your side. Your message should be *understood* clearly by the listener. Communication is complete when the message you deliver is received by the recipient and then the recipient gives a feedback to you. However, it is a sad truth that most of us are practising only 50% of communication because we do not take feedback. Neither do we ask for feedback, nor are we open to feedback even when we get it without asking. Just because we are teachers does not mean that we are only supposed to speak to be able to complete the communication process. We have to be open to feedback as well.

As we saw earlier, in the Johari Window, to be able to evolve we need to be open to feedback. My general observation so far has been that, instead of effectively communicating, I see a lot of teachers get into power struggles with one another, with the parents, and often with the children as well. The need to prove yourself right becomes most powerful. Then you start communicating as if to win the argument and prove that you are right and the other person is wrong. Thus, the very purpose of effective communication gets defeated.

You have become a teacher by choice and not by chance. Therefore, to make a difference through this role of yours, you must make the best use of this beautiful tool called effective communication. To become a successful teacher, you will have to work with all the three groups.

Effective Communication with Children

1. Children have unconditional faith and belief in their teachers. They have great respect for them. The teacher's word is the final word for them and gets lodged in their subconscious minds for life. So dear teachers, be extremely careful of what you speak and how you address and interact with them because they will get impacted by each and every word uttered by you.
2. While addressing them in public, always focus on their strengths. When you have to give them a critical feedback, do it in private.
3. When an incident is reported, always look at all the puzzle pieces before jumping on to any conclusions because children can be manipulative at times.
4. Treat each student as a unique individual, respect each one, and respect their point of view.
5. Validate the feelings of the children of your class. It will help them develop a bond with you because you are making an effort to acknowledge their feelings.
6. Whenever you are communicating with them, you must always stick to "I" statements, for example, "I feel this is how this situation must be dealt with. However see how you would like to go about it."

7. Never ever compare your students among themselves or with others. Instead, help them believe in their own, unique abilities.
8. Always have unconditional faith and belief in your students, which you must express to them often.
9. And yes, please have realistic expectations from them, because unrealistic expectations create undue pressure on them.
10. Whenever you are appreciating a particular student, always appreciate the process, not the child. For example, if a child has scored full marks in a test, you can say, "I am so proud of your hard work," rather than, "You are an excellent girl."
11. Talk to them about other things in their life besides studies. Please find time to listen to their concerns and guide them appropriately.
12. The best way of communication with your students is to become an empathetic listener. When they come to you to share something, give 100% of your attention. Just listen to them without being judgmental, without attempting to give them a solution or without being critical of the situation. This practice alone will go a long way in becoming effective teachers.
13. Always have an eye contact with your children whenever you are communicating. This is an important aspect of effective communication between any two individuals.
14. Address students with their names while communicating with them.
15. We, as teachers, must never ever indulge in labelling children, because these labels get stuck to them and become a part of their personalities for life; they actually start living by the labels.
16. Create an open and positive communication climate in your class where every student feels free to express their true feelings without any hesitation.

17. Last, but not the least, you do not have to shout if you have entered a chaotic classroom and your presence is not getting recognized. Just stand there and start having eye contact with every student. Everything will fall in place in about five minutes without you uttering a single word.

Effective Communication with Parents

1. A teacher is incomplete without parents. And parents are incomplete without the teachers, because parents and teachers are the two important pillars, the two significant adults who share the child. Therefore, to bring out the best in the child, teachers need to collaborate with parents and walk hand in hand with them.

    I need to emphasize on one point here—please use your role as a teacher judiciously. In my 25 years plus career in this profession, I have seen that the moment someone becomes a teacher, they start feeling that they are in power. They feel they are on the giving end. The feel that the parents are on a lower level and they are on the receiving end. Parents should be treated as equal collaborators and you should work as a team with them.
2. When you become a teacher, you not only need to take care of the children, but you also need to take care of the parents. There has to be a connection between the home and the school. You need to take care of the parents also because the children spend 80% of their time at home— so you have to give due importance to the members at home who contribute to the home environment so meaningfully. In fact, if you want the best for the children of your class, you have to collaborate with their first teachers, who are their parents.
3. Like any other relationship, parent-teacher relationship is also a very sensitive one. First of all, treat parents as equals. You are in a service industry and parents are your

clients. You must respect them and give them importance and respect.

To help parents develop trust and faith in you, in the first quarter of the academic year, give a "care" call to all the parents. You can call them up and say, for example, "Hello, Mrs Bhasin. I am Monika, your daughter Riya's class teacher. I must say it's such a pleasure to have Riya in my class. She is a very well behaved girl and is very helpful. I would be glad if you could tell me something about Riya so that I can get to know her better." Can you imagine how great this parent is going to feel? Now, if you have to call this parent for a concern any time, even after six months, there will be so much openness and receptivity in this relationship that your work will be much easier.

As teachers, you are not going to work in isolation. You have to collaborate with the parents. So it is a good idea to develop a great bond and trust with them in the first quarter itself.

4. However, be professional at all times. Do not become over-friendly with the parents. Remember, you share a professional relationship with them, not a personal one. Never talk against your organization or any other staff member.
5. Whenever you have to meet them, have a planned meeting. Do not entertain mini PTMs at the pick and the drop time. Never talk to the parents in the corridor or while you are standing. Please sit comfortably and then talk to them.
6. Whenever there is a concern about the child which you want to share with the parents, always talk about 3 or 4 positive traits of the child first. Then talk about the concern. Always add, "Because I care about Rahul (use the child's name) and I am really concerned, so I thought of discussing this matter with you." Involve the parent.

I Need to Communicate to Relate 73

Tell the parent, "This is what we have evaluated in the school. However, I would like your opinion. Please give us more inputs because you know your child better than anyone else."

7. Compliment the parents for their hard work. You can carry those small sized cards, where you can write compliments and give to the parents. This will go a long way in building your relationship with them, because no one ever tells the parents that they are doing a great job, or that they are involved parents. Acknowledge the efforts that parents put in by comments like, "Keep it up! You are investing quality time in your child; You understand your child's emotions so well; You are so regular in all the Parent Teacher collaboration programs; You are a caring Parent; and so on."

8. Many parents would require handholding, guidance and regular counselling. Please understand your responsibility and take the parents along this beautiful journey. Remember, you are here to make a difference.

9. If the parents need your support, guidance or help, please provide it. Remember, each satisfied parent is going to talk positively about you and the school to 10 other parents.

10. Do not ever label parents and form biased opinions about them. Give them respect. Do not compare them with one another because each of them is a unique individual.

11. For a great relationship with parents, you need to listen to them with empathy, without judging, giving solutions or critically analysing. You will find that most of your concern will be resolved just with this.

12. Always involve the parents and take inputs from them regarding their children. Acknowledge their efforts and make them believe that they are an integral part of the learning and evolution process of their children.

13. If there is any error from your side or if there has been any communication gap, it will be a great thing to apologize. After all, teachers are also human beings. It is normal to make mistakes, but it is much better to accept them. Do not get into the mode of being defensive and putting all the blame and responsibility on parents or someone else. Always see parents as collaborators and not as someone who is pitched against you.
14. If you come across anxious parents, then understand the fact that their behaviour is coming from their past or childhood days. Make a little extra effort to help them and calm their anxiety. Over a period of time, it is likely that they will feel more comfortable.
15. There is no one method to handle all parents. Handle each as per the need.
16. Never talk to a parent negatively about their child in front of other parents or teachers. It is a must that you discuss their child individually and not in front of others, which may embarrass them.
17. Whenever you are meeting the parents, always ask them how their journey has been so far and how is their child doing. Always be open to any feedback from them and make a note of it. Most of the times parents only want empathy and just want to be heard.

Effective Communication with Co-Teachers and Other Staff Members

1. When you become a teacher, you are constantly under observation, so be professional when you communicate with anybody during your official time.
2. Treat your colleagues with respect. Be empathetic towards them. Always accept different point of views—it is healthy to differ from one another.
3. Talk only when required; try to listen more.

4. If you ever face a conflict, make an attempt to talk to that person in private and clear the misunderstanding.
5. Never shy away from complimenting people for their strengths, hard work and their ideas.
6. Always take feedback gracefully, whether it is negative or positive. Do not get into a defensive mode. It's not about proving anyone right or wrong. Instead, reflect on the feedback given and based on that, work on the area of improvement and evolve as a person.
7. Do not discuss and dissect the personal and professional lives of people. Concentrate on your own growth and development.
8. Share ideas; do not hide them from your colleagues.
9. Do not ask personal questions if the other person is uncomfortable. It is great to concentrate on your professional roles and ask questions related to that. And be professional, do not try to become personal friends. It is best to keep personal and professional life separate.
10. Transform energy. When your colleague says something that hurts you, do not respond tit-for-tat. Do not absorb the negativity and start sulking. Instead, transform the energy and direct it to your colleague. Say an affirmation like, "I know my friend very well. She is a pure and peaceful soul. I know that her intention was not to hurt me." Thus send a lot of peace vibrations to her. Believe me, it really works—I have been applying this on myself, with great success.
11. Do not join the group when people are talking negatively about life and situations. Instead, show them something positive. Remind them to count their blessings and bring them back on track.

7

Let Me Follow My Intuition

Trusting our intuition often saves us from disaster.

Anne Wilson Schaef

What is intuitive teaching? This is one question whose answer I took a long time to discover. In my several hundred interactions with teachers all across India, I have asked this question to teachers who are about to retire, teachers who have been around for as long as 10–15 years, teachers who have just begun their teaching career and also adults who are about to embark on their journey as teachers, that is, trainee teachers. Till recently, I had not been able to get an answer which could satisfy my curiosity about who an intuitive teacher is.

This quest to understand intuitive teaching came to an end when I came across some incidents related to teachers and children.

> About five years ago, I got a frantic call from a parent. She wanted to meet me urgently and requested for an appointment. The appointment was fixed with this mother, who also happened to be a medical doctor. When we started the discussions, she almost had tears in her eyes. She said, "Ma'am, I need help. Please tell me where I am going wrong in my parenting practices. My 3 year old daughter is unable to write her numbers and alphabets on the sheets which are being sent by the school." The mother said that because of these sheets, she was also questioned by her husband, "What are you doing with the child? You left your private practice so that you could invest your time in the child and now our child cannot even finish this simple sheet sent by the school!"

Somehow I pacified the mother and told her that she was doing a brilliant job as a parent. She should relax and not become too anxious that her child was unable to write the numbers and the alphabets on the practice sheet sent by the school. I explained that when we send a practice sheet on the weekend, we don't want that the parents should force their child to complete the sheet. They should just give the sheet to the child and let him or her do as much as they can. Because every child is unique and each one of them is different, when it comes to their achievement milestones, there is a lot of difference in the chronological and the mental age of different children. So she should not force her child to finish the sheet. Through my counselling session, I assured her that she and her child were absolutely normal. She should not worry nor be anxious. She should not pressurize the child at all.

The next day I got a call from another parent.

The parent said that she wanted an urgent appointment to discuss her son's progress. The situation was similar. However, here the mother had started pressurizing the child so much so that the child had started crying on the very mention of school. In addition, the mother had used the teacher as a bogeyman by saying, "If you don't finish your practice sheet, I will call your class teacher." Since then, the child had completely refused to go to school. He would start crying in the middle of the night. It was then that she sought this appointment.

This was again a pre-nursery child, less than three years old. After pacifying the mother, I explained to her how unfortunate it was that in her anxiety, she compelled the child to do something which he was not capable of. Subconsciously, the child started associating the pressure and unrealistic expectations with school and the teacher. Since all children want to avoid pain and pressure, because of this association, the child started crying at the very mention of the teacher and the school, to the extent that he refused to go to school altogether.

I gave her strategies how to help the child. He had to be helped to disassociate school with pressure by not forcing him to do the sheets if he did not want to do them. I explained that she should never ever use the teacher as a bogeyman. Instead, it would be helpful to say, "School is fun and your teacher loves you unconditionally."

The next day I decided to interact with all the teachers of pre-nursery classes. When I saw the practice sheets, I realized they were impossible for pre-nursery children to do. My next question was, why were they given? So I went to the teachers of the two pre-nursery children whose parents had sought urgent counselling because of these unrealistic practice sheets. The teachers said that the sheets were given to the children on the instructions of one of the senior teachers.

All the teachers of the various sections of the pre-nursery told me that they had given the practice sheets to the children. With pride in their eyes they showed me how beautifully most of their children had done the sheets. On seeing these sheets, I could immediately see that baring two or three, the rest of the sheets were not appearing to be the children's work. So either the parents had done them or, as parents often do in such situations, they had held the hand of the child and made them write.

However, when I went to the last class and enquired about these practice sheets, the teacher said, "Ma'am, I have not got the sheets printed or given to the children." My immediate question to her was, "Why haven't you done something which was given by a senior and which has been completed by all the other sections of pre-nursery?" She replied, "I know my children and their achievement milestones. These sheets are impossible for pre-nursery children to do." Since she felt that these sheets were inappropriate for her children, she took the decision of not circulating and sending them home with them.

I was very happy and impressed. Among this large crowd of teachers, there was at least one who had applied her common sense and intuition and had saved the children of her class and their parents the ordeal which all the other sections were going through. I call this teacher as an intuitive teacher, who, because of intuitive teaching practice, could support the children and parents of her class by not following blindly whatever the masses were doing.

Finally, I had found the true example of an intuitive teacher.

As teachers, apply your intuition in every situation. Think about everything before you implement it. Try and analyze if what is expected out of the children is age-appropriate. If it looks unrealistic to you, do not implement it unmindfully.

I can understand it will not be easy, but make a genuine effort to give your feedback to the team or the seniors and your views on how you feel it could be done differently. Since your intention is to have realistic expectations from the child, it is likely to be appreciated. Many a times incorrect actions happen just because nobody looked at the situation from the point of view that you may be expressing. So go ahead and express your concern in a calm and logical manner. This practice of yours will save the children of a lot of struggle and torture that they unknowingly get subjected to.

8

I Need to Teach to Reach

If a child can't learn the way we teach, maybe we should teach the way they learn.

Ignacio Estrada

It is extremely important to teach in such a way that you can reach each and every child of your class. Reflect back to your school days. Think about your favourite teachers and your favourite subjects. Why did they become your favourite subjects? Because you enjoyed that class and you enjoyed the company of that teacher. Today, to be successful in making a difference to your students, you, too, have to create the same interest in your class.

Here are some points which must be kept in mind while explaining a particular concept to children:

1. Before presenting any concept, create disequilibrium in the minds of children. When you create disequilibrium between the environment and the learner, the immediate response is curiosity, which will help the learner in restoring equilibrium by acquiring knowledge about the concept which is being introduced.

Suppose you have to introduce red colour to children. You can set up a provocation before the children enter the class by keeping a nicely decorated magic box which only has items which are red in colour. You can also have a magic wand next to the magic box. Can you imagine what will happen when you enter the class? You are likely to see that all the children are standing around the magic box with curious looks and many questions, "Ma'am what is in this box? What are you going to do with this magic stick?" That is the time you can tell them, "Today we will have a magic show in the class." Then you can use the magic wand and whatever you take out from the magic box will already have the attention of all the children and so they will readily absorb the concept given by you.

2. Always introduce the concept in such a way that you can cater to all the three major learning styles prevalent in children – visual, auditory and kinaesthetic. A typical class will have a mix of all the three types of students. There will be some who learn through observation, there will be some who learn through listening and talking, there will be some who will learn through movement, that is, by exploring. So whatever may be the concept, you can first narrate a story to cater to the auditory learners, then show a video for the visual learners and then plan a movement activity to cater to the needs of kinaesthetic learners.
3. In a typical class, there will always be children who are at the same chronological and mental age. For example, if by age they are 7 years old, their mental age will also be 7. However, there will be some children who are at a higher mental age, that is, their mental age might be 8 or 9 years. And there will be some children who might be at a mental age of 5 or 6 years. Therefore, while making a lesson plan, you will have to take care of all the three categories. You will be required to make three lesson plans for any concept – the first plan can cater to the group of children who have the same mental and chronological age; the second plan can cater to the children who have a higher mental age and the third can cater to children whose mental age is lower than the chronological age. So apart from one base lesson plan, there will be two more contingency plans.

However, in regular practice, teachers make only one lesson plan, which might not meet the needs of all the children in the class.

Remember, teachers, that the children who have a higher mental age than the chronological age are the ones who, unfortunately, become a challenge for the teachers. At times they are called hyperactive. I would request you not to use such negative labels to address them. Instead, you can address them as "super energetic children". And if your concern as a teacher is how to handle super energetic children, it's a reflection on your planning. If you have a contingency plan ready, then you can engage them constructively. These children will be able to finish their task quickly. If you are not able to engage them meaningfully, they will engage in some activity which might disturb the class and the other children. The children who have mental age lower than the chronological are the ones who require handholding. It would be a great idea to pair them with the super energetic ones as their task buddies.

4. Always take the children from the known to unknown. For example, if you have to teach children about extinct animals, you will have to talk to them first about animals in the immediate environment, like dogs, cats, goats, which are domestic animals, then talk to them about wild animals and then talk to them about how, as time progressed, those animals which could not evolve and adjust with the changing environment, became extinct.

5. While explaining a concept, always remember to take the children from simple to complex. For example, if you want to explain the concept of the world to your children, you will have to begin from simple things like me and my family, then talk of my city, then my country and then the world.

6. Always remember to take the children from a concrete concept to an abstract concept. Try to concretize your concepts as much as possible. Children learn quickly with concrete experiences. This is the reason why some children find it difficult to understand numbers and alphabets. It is for the simple reason that these are abstract, so they take a long time to get registered. When you make the numbers and alphabets concrete so that the children can feel them and relate to them from their daily experiences, then it becomes easy for them to understand and retain the concept.

Remember, dear teachers, for a particular class the curriculum is the same, but how each one of you presents it totally depends on you. That is what makes all the difference to the process of learning. With your creativity and imagination, you have to make the presentation of the curriculum so interesting that all the children in your class can get engaged and enjoy the process of learning, as well as readily absorb the concept. In case you still find that there are children who have concerns, then you must ask for the intervention of a school counsellor or a special needs teacher so that they can observe the child, understand his or her requirements, and prepare a suitable intervention plan.

Remember, dear teachers, that observation is your most effective tool, with the help of which you can truly make a difference to the lives of your students. For children who are facing learning difficulties, if the intervention happens in the early years, they will be able to cope in a much better way. Therefore, teach so well that you can reach each and every child in the class.

9

Let Me Be a Story Teller

The most powerful person in the world is the story teller. The story teller sets the vision, values and agenda of an entire generation that is to come.

Steve Jobs

Story telling is the most important teaching aid in the hands of a teacher. You can explain even the most difficult of concepts in a story form. Children will easily understand the concept and retain it for a life time. Human brain is wired to listen to stories and children can absorb and retain difficult concepts through stories.

The great news is that teachers are born story tellers and the greatest of all story tellers have been the best teachers since times immemorial.

Our history is a witness to stories being the best form of teaching. In fact, stories from Gita and Mahabharata inspire us till date. We, as children, have all grown up on a very healthy and nutritious diet of stories. And in those stories we, as children, found answers to almost all the questions, including how we came into existence, what is life and what happens after life.

Stories have been our most solid foundation and have shaped our personalities. Stories have an unconditional control and command on us and have been our guiding light through our personal journeys. We, human beings, cannot resist stories because they activate our imagination and creativity and we follow the beautiful movie created in our minds.

I began my teaching profession with the reflection of my student days. I could easily remember all the stories that my teachers had shared with me. As a student also, my preference for attending a class would be based on the number of stories narrated by the teacher. I always found English and Biology the most interesting, because my teachers in these two subjects had many stories to tell,

Let Me Be a Story Teller

> which made the subject and the content very interesting. Therefore, I decided to make stories an integral part of my teaching style.

I always begin my class with a story. If required, I also use stories in-between as well. And my students remember all the stories and the concepts. The takeaways from the stories are always fresh in their minds.

Mentioned here are some of the most important reasons why stories should be an integral part of your teaching practice:

1. Story telling is motivating because it helps children visualize and imagine. Albert Einstein said, "Imagination is more important than knowledge, yet too often this essential part of education is ignored at home as well as in school." Imagination helps us solve problems and help us to think out of the box.
2. Story telling impacts all the areas of development and has a holistic impact on the child.
3. Story telling helps in contributing and increasing knowledge in children and engages reluctant learners.
4. Story telling enhances listening skills in children.
5. Story telling introduces new vocabulary to children.
6. Children of all age groups love stories and it is a great tool for sharpening their memory.
7. Through stories we can remove blinkers and help children broaden their mental horizon.
8. Story telling helps in understanding self, and helps in understanding others.
9. Whenever you are using story telling as a tool to explain an important concept, you instantly tap into the emotions and feelings of children, which helps you to convey a deep message based on emotions.

10. Whenever you are imparting concepts through stories, the embedded concept in that story gets transferred to the subconscious mind of the students and stays there forever, guiding them from time to time, whenever they face a similar situation.

Mentioned here are some of the ways in which you could make story telling a part of your daily teaching:

1. Narrate your own personal stories. When you incorporate your own personal stories, you motivate your children, empathize with them and tell them that even you have gone through the situations that they are going through. For example, talk to them about how you got punished outside the class, how you were misunderstood by your teachers, how you experienced failures and successes and how you learnt important lessons through these experiences. This will help you build a strong emotional connect with your students, because through your personal stories they will know that you can relate with them, understand their challenges and empathize with their issues.

2. Begin your class with a story to create disequilibrium, thereby engaging the curiosity of the children and their attention.

3. You can also weave a story around the concept you are explaining. This will make understanding it easy for them. Stories are so engaging that the children, who might otherwise find it difficult to relate to abstract concepts, might get interested due to the element of curiosity in the stories. Whenever you use a story to explain an important concept, you instantly tap and connect with the emotions of the child, which makes learning permanent.

4. Use role play as a story telling method, where you can have the students act out the whole concept. This is sure to attract the attention of all present. In this way, you are also reinforcing the concept once again.

5. Use case studies as an integral part of your teaching. Case studies are nothing but stories. They present real life situations, challenges, conflicts, and problems, which the characters encounter and have to overcome. This gives an insight to students to handle people and situations. A good case study, according to Professor Paul Lawrence, is "the vehicle by which a chunk of reality is brought into the classroom to be worked over by the class and the instructor." A good case study, about some stubborn facts that must be faced in a real life situation, keeps the class discussion grounded.
6. Use interactive story telling. Pick up stories that can readily engage your listeners so that they actually become the participants in the story.
7. Make difficult and complicated stories your own. Tell these stories in your unique way, and use your personal style to make them effective.
8. Build a story telling environment in your class. Invite students to share small stories. You, too, should share your small life stories to make the class more interesting and meaningful.
9. Encourage pair and group story telling. Make pairs and groups in your class. Give the children the "big idea" and let them weave a story around it. The students can then narrate their stories in pairs and groups so that their anxiety levels, of individual performance, become low. Then the children can readily share their stories.
10. Incorporate "talk story" into the classroom. Talk story simply means an informal chat, where the teacher chats with the students on any and every thing like past events, past experiences, personal conversations, family conversations, and so on. Every child is a born talker so they get readily absorbed in a talk story.

There are no right or wrong ways of incorporating stories in your lesson plan. As a teacher, you have to figure out what works for you.

10

I Need to Be a Thorough Professional

Professionalism is an attitude, not a time commitment.

Deb Bixler

The moment you become a teacher, you are a professional and you must become conscious about this aspect of your personality. All organizations expect their employees to follow a professional code of conduct. When it comes to the teaching profession, the expectation becomes all the more serious and plays a major role in your growth and evolution as a teacher.

Mentioned here are some do's and don'ts of being a thorough professional:

1. Keep your personal and professional lives separate. You must know how to switch on and switch off to be able to maintain a balance between your personal and professional roles. The moment you step out of your house, switch off your personal mode and switch on your professional mode. The moment you get back home, do the reverse. Do not indulge in any gossip sessions about your personal life, neither with your colleagues nor with the children or their parents. You should never take the problems of your school back home to bother your family members. By indulging in this practice, you will be simply magnifying the problems, not solving them at all.

2. Dress appropriately, according to your role as a teacher. The outfit should not be too flashy or loud or over stimulating, because it may become a source of distraction to children and parents alike. The way you carry yourself should be such that it conveys professionalism.

3. As a responsible teacher, do not absent yourself without prior information, unless there is an emergency which cannot be avoided. There is a lot planning and reorganization required even if a single teacher takes leave.

4. Manage your time smartly. Prepare and plan in the evening itself what will you wear the next morning for school. Also organize other things at home so that you can reach your workplace well in time. Always be punctual. Respect your time and also respect the time of others. Make a "to do" list daily to help you guide through the day.
5. Do not indulge in any kind of groupism. Work collaboratively as a team, since all of you have a common goal.
6. Practise healthy and hygienic washroom ethics. This is one of the most basic of all human habits, but unfortunately, as per my observations, this is the most neglected one.
7. Communicate clearly, and during the process talk less and listen more. Speak only when actually required.
8. Be always open to feedback from the children you teach, from your colleagues and from parents. Remember, we are all in the process of learning and evolving; we are not finished products.
9. Practise empathy with all the people you interact with at your work place.
10. Maintain a decent distance from the parents you interact with, which means, do not develop any friendship with them at a personal level. Never ever discuss your personal problems with them.
11. Maintain a professional relationship with your colleagues. It is highly advisable not to have any kind of personal relations with them. This will save you from a lot of unnecessary emotional problems.
12. If you are at fault at any time, please do not hesitate to admit it. We are all human beings and can make mistakes. It is absolutely OK to make mistakes. But it is more courageous to accept your mistakes and make amends.

13. You are a role model, so exhibit appropriate behaviour always, whether you are interacting with children, parents, colleagues or support staff. Give due respect to everyone. Use suitable language to communicate.
14. As a teacher, always make sure that your classroom is fully equipped with all the required material for facilitating the process of learning in children. Also, please make sure you always have a functional first aid box.
15. Give compliments to the children you teach, their parents, your colleagues and support staff. This will act as a great support for a healthy, professional relationship. The bond among the team members will become stronger. Remember, nobody works alone; people need other people to function in a professional set up.
16. Do not ever reach any conclusions by only seeing one half or a part of the picture. Make the effort to go into the entire details. Put all the pieces together to see the whole picture. Only then reach a final conclusion.
17. Be a problem solver. Whenever you need to approach your seniors with a problem, always brainstorm in advance and have multiple solutions or options ready before you take your problem to them. So discuss the problem with them, but be ready to propose multiple solutions. Remember, organizations prefer to have problem solvers rather than problem creators.
18. Stay away from rumours. Do not believe them—you have not heard the other side.
19. Do not ever indulge in any kind of business or direct selling at your workplace. Remember, your workplace is not supposed to be your client market and your organization will never appreciate this.
20. Always be proud, happy, and have a pleasant smile. As a teacher you are the chosen one, who can truly make a difference to the lives of your children and become a tool to change this world for the better.

I Need to Be a Thorough Professional

21. Express gratitude to God by practising affirmations given in the last chapter. Remain positively focussed whenever you are feeling low or are having doubts or any kind of confusion.
22. When you are in the process of leaving your organization, do not ever try to negatively influence the minds of the other teachers there. This is your individual journey, so go through a positive transition; don't choose negative behaviour.
23. Even when you have left the organization, do not ever talk negatively about it. This is not considered professional at all and this practice of yours might impact your career in the new organization.
24. Remember, change is the only thing that is permanent. So embrace all the changes gracefully and have a wonderful, fulfilling life as a teacher.

Remember, dear teachers, that organizations prefer teachers who are professionals. Teachers who are self-aware have the ability to take up challenges, are proactive, are open to learning, know how to handle people and situations, are imaginative and creative, can think out of the box, always catch the attention of the employers. It is a fact that nobody in an organization has the time or patience to teach you skills from scratch. So you have to practise all of the above and be a thorough professional.

11

Let Me Practise Affirmations

We cannot always control our thoughts, but we can control our words and repetition impresses the subconscious mind and we are then master of the situation.

Florence Scovel Shinn

I have been a major practitioner of using affirmations in my daily life, both on the professional as well as the personal front, for which I thank Louise L. Hay. I have experienced many large, positive impacts of affirmations, which have helped me sail through my journey till now. So I am really excited to share this immense power of affirmations with you, dear teachers.

Affirmations are positive statements which we need to practise regularly. This can either be done by writing them down or by reading them. Affirmations impact the conscious and the subconscious mind. When we use affirmations, the words used for affirmations automatically and subconsciously help us to create mental images in the mind, which energize, inspire, and motivate us. The use of affirmations is very beneficial for each one of us in a number of ways. Some of these are mentioned below:

1. By the regular use of affirmations we remain positively motivated.
2. Affirmations help us to remain focussed on our goals.
3. Affirmations stimulate the subconscious mind and help us maximize its power.
4. Affirmations help us to work on our TEA system, that is, our Thoughts, Emotions, and Actions.
5. Positive words used in affirmations empower and energize us to help us in transformation and in our journey of life.

Affirmation for Me, the Teacher

I am the teacher and I am here by choice.
Teaching is my beautiful sense of purpose.
And I am here to make a difference to the lives of my students!
I am ready to change and reinvent myself,
Because I know for sure that I have the power,
To impact a child for life!
I will take utmost care of my physical, mental and emotional health.
With my morning cup of tea, I will check my TEA system daily,
And will keep it in place.
And I will program my mind daily, first thing in the morning.
As success is my birthright,
I will keep the bucket of my self-esteem always full.
I will leave no stone unturned to nourish my resilience and emotional quotient.
And I will always keep my stress levels absolutely low.
I will from now on only focus on solutions and not problems,
And I will always think out of the box.
I love and believe in myself, unconditionally,

And therefore I will always value myself and daily spend "me" time with myself.
I will always please myself first, instead of only pleasing others.
I will always be open to feedback, especially the critical ones.
Because I know for sure that they are the ones to help me to evolve.
Reflection and evolution are my basic nature,
I am a reflective, evolutionary practitioner,
For I am the teacher and I am here by choice.
I promise to make a difference to the lives of the children I teach,
I am a teacher and I am here by choice!
Teaching is my beautiful sense of purpose,
And I am here to make a difference to the lives of my students!

Affirmations for the Children I Teach

I am a teacher and I am here by choice, to make a difference!
I love all my children alike,
I love each one of them for their uniqueness,
I love all that they are good at,
I always catch them for their positive behaviours,
For I know that when I give attention to their positive behaviour, it is likely to grow.
I love my children, so I always appreciate them in public,
But I always give them critical, constructive feedback in private.
And I always tell them that because I love you and because I care for you,
So I feel you could try this, see if you would like to try.
I love my children and so I listen to each of them,
I always get down to their level, have an eye contact with them and then validate their feelings.
I love my children, so I always empathize with them,
I love my children, so I never ever judge them,
I love my children, so I never ever compare them,
I love my children, so I always teach them from the bottom of my heart,

I love my children and have unconditional faith and belief in each one of them,
And I know for sure that each of them will blossom at their own pace!
I am proud of each of my children!
I am a teacher and I am here by choice, to make a difference!

Affirmations for My Organization and My Colleagues

I am a teacher and I am here by choice,
And I am here to make a difference!
I love my organization and I am thankful to my organization for giving me this wonderful opportunity.
I love my organization for their faith, belief and trust in me.
I love the colleagues I work with,
I have unconditional positive regard for each one of them.
I have a beautiful relationship with each one of them,
We are all here to work collaboratively for our common purpose.
I love my colleagues, so I always have a heart-to-heart talk with them to clear our emotional and communication blockages.
I love my colleagues, so I always share my learnings and knowledge with them.
I love my colleagues so I never ever compete with them,
Instead I am only competing with myself.
I love my colleagues, therefore I always give them

constructive feedback and I remain open always for such feedback from them.

I love my colleagues, therefore I never gossip about them behind their back.

I love my colleagues, therefore I work collaboratively with them as a team.

I am a teacher and I am here by choice,

And I am here to make a difference!

Affirmations for the Parents with Whom I Interact

I am a teacher and I am here by choice,
To make a beautiful difference in every child's life!
I have a trusting relationship with every parent I interact with,
For I respect them and they respect me.
I always listen to their concerns with all my attention,
And I always treat all my parents alike.
I never judge any parent, nor do I label them,
And when a parent is overly concerned, I know they are insecure and then I handhold them and guide them and take them through this journey.
I know and value parents as our equal partners,
For I know that the teacher and the parents need to walk hand in hand to bring out the best in every child,
Because the teacher and the parents share the precious child.
I will team up with the parents to maximize every child's learning,
Because I am a teacher and I am here by choice,
To make a beautiful difference in every child's life!

Bibliography

Bay, Brandon, *The Journey*, Harper Element, an imprint of Harper Collins Publishers, 1999

Byrne, Rhonda, *The Secret*, Simon & Schuster UK Ltd., 2006

Cleary, Beverly, *Ramona Quimby Age 8*, William Morrow, 1981

Covey, Stephen R., *The 7 Habits of Highly Effective People*, Free Press, 1989

Covey, Stephen R., *Change Anything*, Business Plus, an imprint of Grand Central Publishing, 2011

Disha, *Because Life Is a Gift*, Shrishti Publishers & Distributors, 2014

Dweck, Dr Carol S., *Mindset*, Constable & Robinson Ltd., 2006

Dyer, Wayne W., *Pulling Your Own Strings*, Arrow Books, 2004

Fensterheim, Herbert, PhD, and Jean Baer, *Don't say YES when you want to say NO*, Dell Publishing, 1975

Goleman, Daniel, *Emotional Intelligence*, Bloomsbury Publishing, 1996

Harris, Thomas A., *I'm OK-You're OK*, Harper Collins, 2004

Hasson Gill, *Mindfulness Pocketbook*, Wiley India Pvt. Ltd., 2015

Hay, Louise L., *You Can Heal Your Life*, Hay House Publishers (India) Pvt. Ltd., 1984

Hesse, Hermann, *Siddhartha*, General Press, 2012

Hill, Napoleon and Judith Williamson, *Thought for the Day*, Jaico Publishing House, 2015

Bibliography

Kulaga, Jaime, PhD, *The SuperWoman's Guide to Super Fulfillment*, Jaico Publishing House, 2016

Lipton, Bruce H., PhD, *The Biology of Belief*, Hay House Publishers (India) Pvt. Ltd., 2005

Mehta, Sneha, *Change Your Life*, Random House India, 2013

Menon, Ritu (Ed.), *Women Who Dared*, National Book Trust India, 2002

Murphy, Dr Joseph, *Maximize Your Potential through the Power of Your Subconscious Mind to Overcome Fear and Worry*, Munjal Publishing House, 2016

Polly. David J., *The Law of the Garbage Truck*, Sterling Publishing Co. Inc., 2010

Tolle, Eckhart, *Practicing the Power of Now*, Yogi Impressions Books Pvt. Ltd., 2012

Tracy, Brian, *Eat that Frog*, Harper Collins Publishers, 2007

Trehan, B. K. and Indu Trehan, *Building Great Relationships*, Sterling Publishers (P) Ltd., 2010

• • •

Books by the same author

This book is meant for all the parents whose children are already going to preschool or are about to start preschooling.

The author shares her tried and tested parenting solutions for young parents, based on her experience of 22 years with parents from all over the country.   ISBN 978 81 207 8765 0

The author, with the help of this amazing collection of 11 parenting stories, touches upon some real, sensitive, and thought-provoking challenges which every parent and child faces today   ISBN 978 81 207 9655 3

Sterling Publishers (P) Ltd.
E-mail: mail@sterlingpublishers.com
www.sterlingpublishers.com